The **Heart of V**

What you can see on the

between Shrewsbury and Swansea,

together with information on some of

the towns and villages along the way

Published jointly by the

Heart of Wales Line Travellers' Association
(HOWLTA) & **KITTIWAKE**

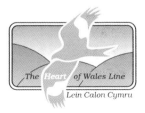

Kittiwake
3 Glantwymyn Village Workshops, Glantwymyn,
Machynlleth, Montgomeryshire SY20 8LY

Published by HOWLTA and Kittiwake
© HOWLTA 2004

Cover photographs of:
Cynghordy Viadict and Dolau © WTB 2004
The Narrows, Knighton by Bill Meadows
Llandrindod Wells by David Perrott

Designed by PerroGraphics, Machynlleth
Printed by WPG, Welshpool on
evolution recycled paper

ISBN 1902302 33 8

A FEW WORDS OF WELCOME

The **Heart of Wales Line** is a public transport service for local people, but for those visiting the area it can be a wonderful travel experience in itself. The aim of this guide is to give you more information about your journey, not only from the train, but also about some of the towns and villages through which the line passes, to encourage you to get off the train and explore.

A visit to the Heart of Wales Line Travellers' Association (HOWLTA) web-site – www.howlta.org.uk – with its many links to other associated sites will, I am sure, give you ideas. Our co-publisher, Kittiwake, produces walks guides, one of which is a compilation of walks from stations along the Line – yet another way to enjoy your journey.

There is a choice of tickets available. A cheap day return is for those who want a day out, but there is also the Heart of Wales Line Circular Ranger which offers a great value opportunity to travel, not only on the HoWL, but also through the English borderlands on the Marches Line. In addition there are Flexipasses which enable you to travel throughout either South Wales or the whole of Wales and the borders by train and bus: both tickets include the HoWL. All these are excellent value and can be obtained from ticket agencies throughout the U.K., including Llandrindod Station Travel Centre (01597 822053).

We are indebted to John Russell who wrote the original draft for the first edition from which much of the information is drawn. It has given me great pleasure to work on this revised and updated second edition and I am very grateful to my committee colleagues and other HOWLTA members who live along the line for all the help they have given me.

No two journeys along the Heart of Wales Line are ever the same and we hope that the guide will inspire you to return again and again in all seasons. A particularly warm welcome awaits those visiting any of the towns, villages or hamlets along the way. We have included information about some of these places to encourage you to get off the train, explore, chat to people and spend money to boost the local economy!

See you on the train!

Gillian Wright
Chairman
Heart of Wales Line Travellers' Association

Introduction to the
Heart of Wales Line Travellers' Association

HOWLTA was established in 1981 by a group of volunteers to provide support for the line and is now one of the largest rail users' groups in the UK. The association works with the train operating company, Arriva Trains Wales, to encourage use of the route by local people and tourists; improve bus/rail connections; monitor service levels and lobby for improvements; run special events and trips from the line and publish a quarterly newsletter.

We hope that you will be encouraged by your journey, both through the following pages and on the train, to become a member of the Association.

Individual membership costs just £4.00, but if you wish to join as a family or you live overseas, the subscription is £6.00. We would be delighted to hear from you and you can send your details, together with the your cheque or postal order made payable to HOWLTA, to:

The Membership Secretary,
Frankville,
14 Broad Street,
Llandovery,
SA20 0AR.

Of course we would like to have your comments and journey experiences, which, with your agreement, we could share with members through the pages of HOWLTA's newsletter.

We have made every endeavour to ensure that the information in the guide is as accurate as possible, but if you find a mistake or something that has changed since going to press, in order that any changes can be incorporated in subsequent issues please let us know by writing to:

David Edwards (Publicity Officer)
Hafod
32 Hendre Road
Llangennech
SA14 8TG
email: david.edwards5 @which.net

Background to the Guide

The first twenty miles between Shrewsbury and Craven Arms are along the line opened by the Shrewsbury and Hereford Railway Company in 1854. This became part of the line known to railwaymen as the 'North & West' route. The train then travels for 88 miles along what came to be referred to throughout as the Central Wales Line before joining Brunel's South Wales Main Line at Llandeilo Junction near Llanelli for the final 11 miles to Swansea.

The guide points out what you can see from the train on the journey from Shrewsbury to Swansea. Emphasis is placed on the line as it is today whilst also mentioning features of yesteryear. In addition to the railway and its artefacts many other items of general interest are included.

We have used the yellow railway mileposts as a general reference point, indicated by the circled numbers – ❸. For southbound travellers these are on the right hand side of the train between Shrewsbury and Llandeilo Junction near Llanelli. However, it is not essential to sit on that side and we hope that you will find the guide easy to follow whatever your viewpoint. Where appropriate, items have also been defined as being either the UP (right hand) side or the DOWN (left hand) side of the train in the direction of travel from Shrewsbury to Swansea. When travelling northbound, the guide can be used in reverse.

Contents

Key to symbols used

㉜   Indicates mileposts along the line

𝒊   Tourist Information Centre

☎   Telephone number

⇌   Station location

Useful telephone numbers

National Rail Enquiries	08457 484950
Arriva Trains Wales	0845 6061 660
Timetables by post	0870 9000 772
Group Travel	0870 9000 767
Recorded Train Running Information	0870 9000 771
Llandrindod Station Travel Centre	01597 822053

Heart of Wales Line Travellers Association web site:

www.heart-of-wales.co.uk

Loading supplies at Lanwrtyd Wells. Bill Meadows.

What you can see along the Heart of Wales Line

Shrewsbury

The station is situated close to the centre of this historic town. First mentioned in a charter of 901, to the Saxons it was known as Scrobbesbyrig. Street names such as Dogpole and Mardol, Gullet Passage and Grope Lane entice visitors to explore further and the many hotels, pubs and shops make the visit even more pleasurable. Historians are well provided for, with more than 660 listed buildings and landmarks such as the abbey, founded in 1083 and still used as a place of worship and the castle which guards the only land approach to the town and houses the museum of the Shropshire Regiments. Readers of the 'Brother Cadfael' books by Ellis Peters can add to their interest by imagining these places populated by the fictional characters. Riverside walks follow the river Severn as it loops round this medieval town of narrow streets and Tudor buildings. The annual Flower Festival is an additional attraction for thousands of people.

Shrewsbury Station is overlooked by the castle on one side and a prison on the other. It is unusual in that parts of the platforms project on to the rail bridge over the River Severn, which can be seen out of the lefthand side window as the train pulls away, but the main item of railway interest is on the **DOWN** side. Here, in a triangle of lines, is the Severn Bridge Junction signal box, one of five boxes in the area. This is the largest remaining manually-operated box in Britain, although fewer than half its original 180 levers are still functional. The line to the left leads to Wolverhampton. The third line of the triangle sees occasional use by freight and charter trains.

DOWN: Shrewsbury Abbey. The site of the once extensive Coleham Locomotive Sheds and yard has been redeveloped. Sutton Bridge Junction signal box controls the junction with the single track Cambrian Line to Aberystwyth (**UP**) and is one of the five boxes in the area. The others are Crewe Junction box, north of the station, Abbey Foregate box on the Wolverhampton line, Shrewsbury Crewe Junction, and Crewe Bank. The former Severn Valley Railway to Bridgnorth used to pass behind the box to the left.

❸ DOWN: Bayston Hill Quarry. Although still connected to the main line, the siding has not seen a train for over ten years (2003).

❹ DOWN: The white house next to the line is the former Condover Station, one of seven closed stations on the first part of the journey.

❻ DOWN: Here is the Dorrington signal box. Industrial units have been built on the old station yard.

❾ DOWN: A builders' yard marks the site of Leebotwood station as the Stretton Hills begin to enclose the line. In the distance is Wrekin Hill with Lawley nearer to the line, followed by Caer Caradoc.

❿ All Stretton Halt was here but no trace remains.

UP: To the west is the Long Mynd with a narrow road, the Burway, following its tortuous route to the summit.

Church Stretton

Nestling in the valley between the Long Mynd and Wenlock Edge, close to Caer Caradoc and Ragleth Hills, the peaceful 18th Century market town of Church Stretton with its Norman church is a popular centre for walkers on the Shropshire Hills. At weekends between Easter and October, minibuses run from the station into the hills to the east and to the west of the railway. For details contact 01588 673893.

⓬ DOWN: Here is a water crane, remnant of the steam era, just ahead of the signal box at Church Stretton. The signals have now been removed and the box is no longer in use.

UP: The original station buildings have survived those which replaced them when the platform was moved to the other side of the road overbridge in 1914. On the platform there is a plaque identifying the precise location of the town as:

Height above sea level 613 feet
Latitude 52 32 *Longitude* 02 48
Real noon 11 mins 12 secs later than Greenwich

This is a reminder that it was the coming of the railways which led to the introduction of Greenwich Mean Time throughout Britain. The train has now climbed over 350 feet since leaving Shrewsbury, on gradients which were a major obstacle to steam trains.

⑭ Diminutive Little Stretton Halt once stood here, beneath the overbridge.

⑮ DOWN: Marsh Brook signal box stands on the north side of a level crossing. The station was to the south.

⑯ DOWN: At Marsh Farm Junction, a single line led in from Much Wenlock. The tree-lined ridge of Wenlock Edge dominates the skyline.

⑱ Site of Wistanstow Halt

⑲ UP: As the train slows for the home signal at Craven Arms the curve of an embankment is just visible to the right. This was Stretford Bridge Junction where the line from Bishops Castle joined the main line. This railway survived for 70 years until it closed in 1935. It was so comprehensively unremunerative that even the legendary Colonel Stephens, saviour of many rural lines, refused to have anything to do with it.

DOWN: The train now stops at Craven Arms Crossing signal box to collect the first of the 'tokens' allowing the driver to proceed along the single track Heart of Wales Line. The token is released under the authority of the signaller at Pantyffynnon, 79 miles away, and guarantees that there are no other trains on the first section of track, the 12 miles to Knighton.

Craven Arms

Following the arrival of the railway in 1850, Craven Arms grew as an agricultural market centre with thousands of animals being transported by train. It is a stepping off point for Stokesay Castle, a wonderfully evocative, fortified manor house which has been quoted as the most photographed building in England. A new attraction is the Shropshire Hills Discovery Centre which follows the story of the creation of the Shropshire landscape from earliest geological times and features a virtual balloon ride over the Shropshire landscape.

UP: The train crosses to the up line for a short distance. In its heyday, this once significant railway town boasted engine and carriage sheds, a goods depot and large station buildings.

⑳ UP: The train leaves the North & West Route immediately beyond the station. Central Wales Junction signal box was here until it was demolished in 1966, leaving the gradient post which stood beside it as an isolated relic, probably the tallest gradient post in the country. The train then negotiates what is reputedly the sharpest curve on a standard gauge passenger line in Britain.

DOWN: On a clear day, the flag on the tower of medieval Stokesay Castle may be glimpsed on the far side of the main line. Your train is now allowed to accelerate up to the maximum 60 mph. The first under bridge spans Watling Street, the Roman Road which here linked the settlements at Wroxeter (*near Shrewsbury*) and Leintwardine (*near Ludlow*). Few people now have cause to journey between these two ancient outposts and parts of the road have fallen under the plough. The very old hedgerow alongside the road near here is still a naturalist's delight.

❶ This first section of the line was built by the Knighton Railway Company and the five overbridges along it are almost identical. The majority of railway crossings have names to assist identification although a number of those on the HoWL have several names. Many of the level crossings on the level have been equipped on both sides of the track with telephones allowing contact with the signal box at Pantyffynnon. If there is a train anywhere in the section the signaller will advise that it is not safe to cross and the call is recorded.

❷ An underbridge takes the B4367 Broome Marsh Road beneath the line. Road traffic has to negotiate the bridge carefully as it needs to make a 'Z' manoeuvre.

Broome

Out of sight of the station is the village pub, the Engine & Tender, which has a handful of railway relics and two idiosyncratic pub signs. The station building was demolished in the great 'rationalisation' programme of the mid 1960s. Wooden-clad and with two huge, brick chimneys, it appeared to stand precariously in mid air over an embankment. Part of the foundations can still be seen from the road below.

UP: The old station house, a stone-built detached and outwardly austere building, indicating that this was not a highly graded posting for a station master, stands on the Aston Road opposite four railway cottages.

Extensions to the former goods shed cannot disguise its original purpose. It has had a variety of uses over the years since the station closed and is now being used by a blacksmith. The steep incline to the yard was a struggle for any steam locomotive, and a shunter's nightmare.

❸ The track now slews from what was the up line to use the former down line and crosses the Clun, the river which links some of the quietest places under the sun: 'Clunton, Clunbury, Clungunford and Clun'. If other Clun villages were omitted from the old Shropshire rhyme that A. E. Housman quoted in his 'A Shropshire Lad', then it can only have been due to poetic metre.

UP: Coston Manor as it is now dates back to the 1850s.

DOWN: The view looking eastwards to Clungunford is pure Shropshire.

❹ This is rabbit territory. Most travellers will probably see a handful, but those on the first train of the day from Shrewsbury are likely to be rewarded with the sight of dozens if not hundreds, though it must be admitted that it is not something entirely appreciated by the farmers. Sunrise on a spring day with a dewy mist makes this early morning train one of the most idyllic travel experiences.

❺ **DOWN**: There was originally a ballast siding on the approach to Hopton Heath. This was followed by an unusual post carrying three signals. Only about three feet of it now remains!

Hopton Heath

The platforms at Hopton Heath were partially staggered, but the down platform is the one now in use. The up platform ended at the overbridge, having extended from opposite the sidings. As at Broome, the only creature comfort nowadays is a three-sided wooden, waiting shelter. The former station house and adjoining bungalow are both privately owned. The '1863' in the brickwork of the house confirms its origins, although the station itself had opened for freight in October 1860 and to passengers in March 1861.

DOWN: Unseen from the train on the station approach road, there is a Pooley weighbridge complete with a stone-built hut. Some of the mechanism has been removed but the hut remains intact in its new role as a superior garden shed.

UP: The location of the first signal box is apparent from a gap under the disused platform for its wires and rods. This box closed towards the end of the Second World War when a new one was opened on the

14

down side close to the sidings. These were unusual in that, although on the down side of the line, access to them was gained only from the up track.

DOWN: The former goods shed stands in a field beside the railway line and beyond it are the chalets of a holiday village and timeshare at Ashley Pools. Remarkably, this is one of the least populated parts of the line – South Shropshire is a delightful place to relax, but this fact is a well kept secret!

Only about 15% of the 90 miles of the HoWL is straight and one of the few stretches of any length starts here.

❻ In the next two miles to Bucknell, the train goes in and out of Herefordshire three times

UP: Bedstone College. The black and white half-timbered building at this independent school dating from 1884 has been painstakingly restored following the severe damage caused by a fire which began on the first day of the school holidays in the summer of 1996.

UP: At Adley Moor the former crossing keeper's cottage lies partially hidden. It has a remote air, although it is not far from the main road.

❼ **UP**: Just before the milepost at Coxhall Farm crossing is another railway relic. Near the path leading from an isolated chapel is a London Midland & Scottish railway boundary post, all the more unusual as the LM&S did not exist until the grouping of railways in 1923. It is sometimes possible to spot some llamas on the hillside immediately beyond the football pitch.

A series of footpath crossings preceding Bucknell station is linked to the village by a picturesque walk alongside the River Redlake.

Bucknell

Within five minutes' walk of the station you can enjoy many enchanting sights in this village, clustered around the River Redlake. Fine walking country, a 16th century schoolhouse and farmhouse and an even older Church, together with tearooms and two welcoming pubs make a stop at Bucknell worthwhile.

DOWN: In the goods yard an old cabin looks as purposeful as the day that it was built. A stone built goods shed dated 1860 is still in daily use by a coal merchant. The Radnorshire Coal Company was started in 1865 by businessmen from Knighton. It had offices at stations from Broome to Llandrindod Wells and elsewhere. Its office is next to another weighbridge and stone hut.

A wood merchant is expanding from the yard to fields at the back, as the conifers planted a generation ago reach maturity. The yard is still busy but none of today's businesses has any direct link with the railway. The former goods platform is just before the crossing and the impressive keeper's cottage.

UP: There is an unusual road sign, depicting a duck – to warn motorists that the wildlife is not so wild around this pleasant village.

❻ UP: This milepost stands at the site of the replacement signal box opened in 1906, the original having been on the south side of the crossing. The heavy wooden crossing gates were removed and the signal box closed in 1978. Road traffic is now controlled only by lights which are activated by southbound trains passing over treadles. These trains stop at the station only on request. Up trains have to stop at the station for the conductor to start the light sequence from a control box on the platform. It is one of seven stations on the HoWL with such a system in operation. Note the continued use of a steam locomotive on road signs warning motorists of an ungated crossing.

DOWN: Current station facilities are limited to a waiting shelter. The station building – now a private house – ranks as one of the most attractive in the country. This is not entirely apparent from the train because it is the patterned roof, gables and chimneys which have turned a plain stone building into a classic country railway station. The row of bungalows is now clad in wood. It is understood that they are amongst the few surviving prefabricated bungalows in the country constructed during the Second World War. The line levels briefly as it leaves the mixed farmland of South Shropshire and enters the heavily wooded hills of the Teme Valley.

UP: The trackless platform has become a feature; on a sunny afternoon one is likely to see a group from the local W.I. tending the flower beds. The former double track-bed is still visible here as the ridges where the sleepers rested are prominent even after almost four decades. Henley Bridge carries Weston Road over the track.

❾ DOWN: The River Teme, which at this point was once the border between England and Wales, meanders close by. The building of the railway has led to the river changing course slightly so river and border no longer coincide. Consequently the line first enters Wales for a few yards at Cubbage. Across the river, Lower Stannage Farmhouse stands above Weston Pit. Gravel was extracted for use as track ballast, but the pit has long since been exhausted. A public footpath now crosses the River Teme via a bridge which was once part of the siding which led to the pit.

Next comes another piece of railway nostalgia: a crossing with double wooden gates on either side of the line. The red of the large wooden circle that warned vehicle drivers of the gates has faded. It is otherwise a perfect example of a type of crossing that has largely disappeared and is now usually seen only on model railways – except that modellers will be disappointed to learn that these gates open outwards, away from the track. They used to allow road access to the gravel pit.

❿ UP: In the narrow field separating rail from lane, dozens of young pheasants may be seen scurrying about. Stowe Bridge gives the hamlet access to the A4113 Ludlow – Knighton road.

⓫ DOWN: The roofs of Knighton can be seen at the start of a seven mile climb, initially at 1 in 200.

UP: *The Lee* is a distinctive house with bartizans (small turrets projecting from a wall) reminiscent of properties in the Scottish Highlands.

Knighton

The station at Knighton is in England, whereas the town is in Wales. It is said that the hotel which stands close by the railway bridge was deliberately built there so as to be in England at a time when Wales was 'dry' on Sundays. Formerly the Central Wales Hotel, it has been renovated after years of deterioration but lost its affinity with the railway when it re-opened as 'The Kinsley'. Explore this hospitable, historic town and include a visit to the Offa's Dyke Centre.

⓬ Tref y clawdd – 'the town on the dyke'

UP: Here once stood a small steam locomotive shed and turntable.

DOWN: Knighton No1 signal box was opposite the shed on the outside of the curve. The stone-built goods shed is now occupied by an agricultural machinery firm. The date 1860 can be seen on a gable end. Alongside the goods shed is a points indicator. Here, nearly thirteen miles from the nearest signalman, the points are hydraulically operated so that they are always set for straight ahead – as at the other passing loops on the line. A train from the opposite direction runs slowly over the points forcing them apart. After the train has passed, they revert to the original position.

The diminutive Knighton No 2 signal box once stood on the platform here.

The station building can claim to be the most impressive on the line, as befits the former headquarters of the Knighton Railway. Stone-built with a mix of tracery, dormer and regular laced windows, it has impressive gables and three substantial chimney stacks. The patterned roof tiles are an outstanding feature. The flat-roofed extension maintains the theme reminiscent of a church, a feeling emphasised by the porch on the front of the building.

The '1860' in a quatrefoil just beneath the gable could almost be an emblem for the birth of the Knighton Railway: the line and station opened for all traffic on March 6th 1861.

As is generally the case with stations, the front of the building is the more impressive, particularly so, in this instance, because the sun seldom shines on the platform side. The building is occupied by a veterinary surgery at present. The variety of agricultural vehicles and appendages at Teme Valley Tractors confirms the intensive and expensive nature of farming these days.

UP: A large water tank stood at the north end of the up platform. Access to this platform is via a narrow footbridge set alongside the road bridge, or by newly installed ramps from the roadway.

The line beyond Knighton to Llanbister Road has always been single track. When the line from Craven Arms was singled in 1965 the up platform line at Knighton was also removed. This made the 31 miles from Craven Arms to Llandrindod Wells the longest single line section in Britain. The passing loop was restored in 1990 and helps in the timetabling of 'special' services such as rail tours.

On arrival at Knighton, the driver goes to a hut to contact the signaller at Pantyffynnon by telephone. The metal token for the section from Craven Arms to Knighton is returned to the token instrument and permission sought to remove the token for the next section to Llandrindod Wells. The journey then continues along what was the original Central Wales Railway.

UP: Note the houses that face the railway rather than the road – originally built as houses for railway staff. Kinsley Wood rises steeply as the train heads north-westwards towards Knucklas. Unseen from the train 'EIIR' was planted in golden conifers amongst the green to commemorate Queen Elizabeth II's Silver Jubilee in 1977.

DOWN: Just visible across the river – at least in winter – is a 'Welcome to Wales' sign, for walkers approaching Knighton along Offa's Dyke Long Distance Footpath.

UP: The Footpath en route between Prestatyn and Chepstow, descends from the hills to cross the line alongside the Teme at Panpunton before continuing through the town.

⓭ Milepost thirteen was certainly unlucky for the fireman of steam trains because it is here that the gradient steepens to 1 in 60 for the five miles to the summit at Llangynllo.

Until the end of steam, banking engines and double-headed trains were a common sight here on heavily laden freight and passenger trains. Banking engines were attached to trains to give extra help on a steep gradient. Those attached at Knighton assisted until Llangynllo.

Having flirted with the Principality four miles earlier and crossed the unofficial boundary a half mile back, the train now finally enters Wales.

DOWN: The mast on Garth Hill, besides being for conventional broadcasting, is also part of the extensive national radio network which enables train crews to communicate with their control centre. Passengers looking back to the south-east at this point should see the Spaceguard Centre on Llanshay Hill. As well as a large telescope it boasts a Planetarium, Camera Obscura and a Seismology unit which was particularly active when there was a tremor here in 1996. It is very well worth a visit.

Another railway relic is found here – a full sized black and white WHISTLE board, one of several which remain on the HoWL. Nearby was the Whitterley Ballast Pit. As at Weston there were sidings here until the turn of the century.

⓮ UP: The River Teme meanders below Skyborry as the line hugs the fringe of Bailey Hill on the south side of the narrow valley. Trotting races take place across the fields at Monaughty Poeth each May.

20

Beyond Knucklas Road overbridge down trains slow to 20 mph, up trains to 10 mph for Lower House Farm Crossing.
UP: Last view of the Teme Valley

DOWN: A water tank is to be seen close to the track. When the line was constructed, it cut across a water course and the tank is there because there is still an obligation to ensure a supply. Whilst it may originally have been to provide a farmhouse with water, sheep are now the chief beneficiaries.

Knucklas

UP: When built, the station house did not have any windows on the north wall away from the railway, thus denying the occupants a superb view. The gradient of 1 in 60 is particularly noticeable if the train stops. Ahead there is a tantalising view of the viaduct and Castle Hill.

⓯ At this point the 'cant' or 'superelevation' – the difference in height between one rail and another – is close to the maximum allowed on Britain's railways at 5 inches. This is necessary because of the sharpness of the approach curve, not the speed of the train.

The contractor for the line was Thomas Brassey, who earlier had built the Shrewsbury and Hereford line. He had also been responsible for constructing the notable line at Balaclava in the Crimea, so the Central Wales route must have seemed a relatively straightforward project. The work was overseen by his partner for the mid Wales area, William Field. The engineer for the line, Henry Robertson, is credited with the design of Knucklas viaduct and the inspirational idea of capping the viaduct to resemble a castle. It would otherwise be a totally unpretentious viaduct across a very minor valley. It is rumoured that it was decided to use the stones from the nearby medieval castle in its construction and one thing led to another.

Be that as it may, the result is that Knucklas has one of the best-known viaducts in Britain. The viaduct is straight and the thirteen stone arches, each spanning 30 feet, take the line 75 feet above the Heyope Valley. The stream of that name passes under the eleventh arch. A minor road passes under the second arch. The castellated turrets at either end of the 190 yard long viaduct are slightly disappointing in that they are hollow and too tall to allow any railman to stand in and pretend to fire arrows or pour boiling oil on enemies!

⑯ DOWN: For the moment, most of the worthwhile views are on this side – including a backward glimpse of the viaduct.

⑰ DOWN: Heyope Crossing Cottage. Even in the frenetic days of steam trains there was never any real justification for a keeper here. The crossing does not straddle a road but only gives access to the steep hillside. The only things to cross the railway were livestock. Eventually, the keeper was made redundant and the farmer was paid for seeing himself and his beasts across.

UP: Beyond Heyope, one hundred yards of well-tended lawn gave access to an unusual water tank. Set high on the embankment the unsightly metal tank was supported on an equally unsightly wooden frame. Water was supplied by a gravity feed pipe. The tank was provided for emergency use in the event of difficulties at Llangynllo. As the hills close in, here is the Upper Cwm Heyope crossing…..then darkness.

⑱ Llangynllo (originally Llancoch) tunnel curves throughout its 647 yards and brings the line through 90 degrees. Glyndwr's Way Long Distance Footpath crosses over the tunnel near to the remaining airshaft which is 80 feet deep.

UP: 200 yards beyond the tunnel, a gradient post marks the highest point of the journey – 980 feet above sea level – as 1 in 100 up becomes 1 in 100 down. The post is not easily seen from the train so passengers may prefer to concentrate instead on feeling the train breast the summit at the railway equivalent of a hump-backed bridge. For comparison, Shap Summit between Lancaster and Carlisle is at 916 feet and

Druimuachdar between Perth and Inverness is at 1484 feet.

Llangynllo

Llangynllo village lies in a valley about a mile distant. 'Cynllo' was one of a quartet of the missionary contemporaries of St. David, the others being Teilo, Padarn and Cewydd. Llangyllo's most recent claim to fame came in 1993 when 'Second Best' starring William Hurt was filmed in the area. Several locals appeared in the film.

UP: Access to the basic platform passes behind the former station house and cottages.
The goods offices and timber hut predate the current shelter. The house was built within a few feet of the track – there cannot be many which are closer. Note the bay window. Llangynllo did not have a traditional signal box and the levers were sited on the ground floor of the house. A water tower, identical to that at Knighton, stood in what is now the garden. The stone base with a large metal tank on top made it as tall as the house.
The 'banking' engines from Knighton, referred to earlier, were detached here and returned to base.

DOWN: The disused platform remains. The barrow crossing between the two platforms is now separated from the station and serves as a farm crossing. Apart from a scattering of farmhouses, few people live in the immediate locality and walkers are the most frequent users of the station.

⑲ The narrow road which has been hugging the line since Knucklas descends steeply to pass beneath it.

UP: A sheer rock face rises where the line has been cut into the hillside at Pye Corner.

DOWN: A solitary tall Scots Pine indicates that drovers once passed this way with their black cattle en route from the Welsh Hills to markets in the Midlands. Traditionally pines were planted to indicate a place suitable for 'bed and breakfast'. Their water supply was the infant river Lugg which rises on Beacon Hill before running into the Wye at Hereford.

⑳ DOWN: Difficult to spot, a road sign here points to four settlements with railway stations: Llangynllo 1 mile, Knucklas 3, Knighton 5, Llanbister Road 2, which illustrates how much the line curves in 8 miles. Those travelling in May can see one of the line's great delights here – masses of bluebells on Maylord Hill, so many you can almost smell them as you pass.

㉑ Troed-y-Rhiwfedwen crossing:

DOWN: Two original wood signs: 'Stop Look and Listen' and 'Shut Gate'. Beyond Maylord Crossing the distance between the lineside fences increases where there was a siding followed by cattle pens and a goods yard ahead of the old double track section.

Llanbister Road

The suffix 'Road' is a railway euphemism meaning that the station is a long way from the place it is said to serve. In this case the 'Road' is also a long way from the road to Llanbister. To all intents and purposes Llanbister Road is a railway hamlet in the same way that Crewe is a railway town. The station was built because of the need to maintain fairly even distances between signal boxes and because of the transition from single to double track at this point. It owes nothing to any desire to serve a distant village on the road between Newtown and Llandrindod Wells.

Though the HoWL was opened as a single track throughout, it was always intended to double most of the route along the easier terrain from here to Llandrindod Wells. This was done promptly, but it was another ten years before it was extended back through the station and the down platform added.

DOWN: An extension to the station house has meant some loss of its identity and the platform has become part of the garden. The habit of marking bricks with the maker's name is as old as brickmaking itself and the names J.Whitehouse and Bloomfield appear frequently here in the blue bricks on the platform edge.

㉒ Cwm-y-Geist overbridge is a substantial dual-width structure apparently leading from and to nowhere but is in fact used to give access to a quarry.

㉓ DOWN: The impressive Bell House. From Llanbister Road the train has been travelling on the former up line but the track slews to the left to take the down line through Dolau. The railway crosses the River Aran twice in a quarter of a mile. The ground here is marshy so cattle are more likely to be seen than sheep.

㉕ UP: A fence protrudes across the former track bed to protect walkers. The bridge which used to take the footpath directly over the river having disintegrated, the path has been diverted to the railway bridge.
What appears to be a pile of rubble disguises one of the great engineering achievements of the late Victorian era – an aqueduct which carries water underground for 73 miles from the Elan Valley to Birmingham. The two pipes are only just below ground level where they pass under the track, but at Fron Tunnel (West) and especially Dolau Tunnel (East) there were major borings.

DOWN: A gradient post, showing '1 in 290/Level' stands, often amidst a myriad of wild flowers, as the train slows to 10 mph for the crossing at Dolau, which is Welsh for 'meadows'.

Dolau

This station has been a frequent winner in its class in the annual nationwide Best Kept Station and other competitions. There was a time when station staff would vie for this honour, but nowadays with stations unmanned, it is left to the local community to maintain the tradition. The winning certificates are displayed in the diminutive chalet-style waiting room along with some poems descriptive of the line. Outside the shelter is one of only two station clocks on the line. In addition to the wonderful flower displays there is a plaque commemorating the visit in 2002 by Queen Elizabeth II during her Golden Jubilee tour of Wales

The station name appears in about five different lettering styles including a Heart of Wales Line sign depicting a Red Kite. There is also a small rail-mounted truck, one of the few remaining artefacts from the standard gauge Elan Valley Railway. This line was built for the construction of the dams and was dismantled when the work was completed.

Down trains stop only on request, up trains have to stop for the crossing. A redundant signal and some railway signs stand in the garden. The signal is not far from home because the garden in which it stands occupies an area where a couple of sidings once trailed from the down line.

UP: Dolau is fortunate in that access to the redundant platform is straightforward and this makes it possible for both platforms to be ablaze with colour in the summer thanks to the efforts of the station Action Group. The train now slews sharply to regain the former up track.

Pen-y-bont Common stretches away to the East.

㉗ DOWN: A few yards from where the River Aran meets the River Ithon, the railway crosses the latter for the first time. A brick wall marks the site of the 'junction that never was'. Pen-y-bont Junction signal box stood here until 1964. It was a junction only insofar as it was the point at which the double track from Llanbister Road reverted to single track through the cutting and tunnel. There had been a plan to extend the Kington Railway over the Central Wales Line from here and on to Aberystwyth. This had fallen through even before the CWL was doubled so the suffix 'junction' may have been used simply to distinguish it from the signal box at the station.

UP: In winter the rock face of the cutting can present an icicle spectacular.

Pen-y-bont Tunnel is 404 yards long, straight and on a gradient of 1 in 74. The double track used to resume beyond the tunnel.

Pen-y-bont

Pen-y-bont village is about a mile east of the station. Its origins date back to its position on the coach road to Aberystwyth. In the village there is a large inn, the Severn Arms Hotel, and annually on the first Wednesday in August, Pen-y-bont is host to the thousands who attend the annual trotting race meeting. The station was named Crossgates when it opened in October 1865 and ironically Crossgates, a mile to the west at the crossroads of the A44 and A483 has since far outgrown Pen-y-bont.

28 **UP**: For many years, four concrete blocks near the shelter served as flower containers and bore the legend 'Safety, Speed, Comfort and Efficiency', an LNWR advertising slogan. No trace remains of the poem which was once inscribed on the steps leading back over the bridge to the main station, but there are plenty of the shells which local children used to bring back before World War II to adorn the station garden when they had been for a day out at the seaside. There is an LMS style station name board, but the yellow has been superseded by black.

DOWN: Amidst the silver birch and scrub that is taking over the disused platform is another ex-LMS station name board. An extensive brick-built station building has been demolished, along with a signal box which stood by the crossing, Beyond that was an extensive yard. The station house and railway cottages survive. Some sheep pens still see active service.

29 **DOWN**: across the fields, Llanbadarn church was rebuilt a century ago, but has Roman ancestry. The second crossing of the River Ithon is only two rail miles from the first but the river has meandered through

27

ten miles of attractive scenery.

㉚ DOWN: A full length whistle board is set well back from what was double track for sighting purposes. It was intended as a warning for Sunnybank Farm Crossing, but Ddole Road overbridge now intervenes and the crossing has been down-graded.

㉛ DOWN: Here, on the outskirts of Llandrindod Wells, there is a distant signal board, the first for 18 miles. The train stops at the level crossing in order for the driver to pull the cord which lowers the double barriers against the road traffic. Until 1986, a signal box controlled operations at the crossing. It closed when the passing loop was moved to the station and the up platform reinstated there.

UP: One of only four remaining sidings on the HoWL. This has been used in recent years to accommodate charter trains visiting the town and special trains for the Royal Welsh Show at Builth Wells, as well as engineering trains.

Llandrindod Wells

The County Town of Powys, Llandrindod Wells parades its Victorian history with pride. There are a number of hotels which owe their origins to the crowds of visitors who descended on the town in the 19th Century to take the waters. An open air market is held on the car park next to the station every Friday.
The signal box has been moved from the level crossing to stand near to where the station box once stood before it closed in 1955. No longer functioning as a signal box, it is now open as a museum on summer Sundays and special days. Visitors are recommended to go below stairs to see how the interlocking operated. The box is painted in the chocolate and cream colours of the Great Western Railway, much to the chagrin of the cogniscenti who have barely recovered from the use of two former Great Western locomotives to haul the Royal Train in 1952. At the time of nationalisation in 1948, Llandrindod Wells became part of the Western Region of British Railways, but it was never a Great

Western station. Originally the colour would have been maroon. Across the road from the up platform and past the Dyfed Powys Police Section Office, is the 16th Century Llanerch Inn. Llanerch was the name of a farmhouse here before the coming of the railway and the expansion of the town, which boasts a lake, several large hotels and the National Cycle Museum.

DOWN: All the goods sidings were here and the former yard is now occupied by an agricultural merchant and a carpark. A goods shed, identical to that at Bucknell, is still in active service as a car showroom. A small compound is used by the line engineers to store items such as temporary speed restriction signs, fishplates, rail keys and other small items needed to keep the line operational. At the point where trains usually draw to a halt, it is possible to step onto a little piece of history. Set in the platform is a slab inscribed: 'This stone from the Claerwen Dam marks the spot where on 23rd October 1952 Queen Elizabeth II first set foot in Wales after her accession to the throne'. A plaque on the building marks the erection in 1990 of an ornate glass canopy which had been removed from the local council offices. This building houses a ticket office, waiting room, clock and toilets. A new footbridge suitable for wheelchair use was erected in 2003.

UP: A direct service to London Euston once departed from this platform. The large, round-topped wooden Victorian post box is one of only two such boxes remaining in Britain. An attractive covering protects it from the elements. It was brought here from Machynlleth and restored.

㉜ A maximum speed of 45 mph applies for the next five miles.

UP: The line crosses Rock Park. A delightful stone underbridge is unseen from the train but it is just possible to spot the path leading down to the springs. Taking the waters at Llandrindod Wells is a unique experience which cannot be replicated elsewhere because the waters do not travel well and should be drunk immediately. A free chalybeate spring still flows in the park.

The train continues through a low, wooded cutting which hides any superficial evidence of the numerous nearby Roman sites shown on the Ordnance Survey map (up) but it cannot hide the A483 which continues to parallel the line (down).

㉝ DOWN: A full whistle board warns of the approach to a rare dual crossing which gives access to two lineside properties. There is one gate on the down side leading from the main road but two independent gates and telephones on the up. Howey is now to all intents a suburb of Llandrindod Wells, but many of the properties here pre-date those of its dominant neighbour.

UP: There is a view across the Wye Valley as a 1 in 74 descent eases. Howey Hall is close to the line, reached by a private road via a rough stone overbridge. A whistle board matches that on the down side for Howey/Greenfields crossing. A road leads to Disserth where, having escaped modernisation, time has stood still at the medieval church.

㉞ DOWN: This section has always been single track but in 1911 a passing loop was added to improve line capacity. At mid loop there was a small signal box but local attempts to have a station built were not successful. When Lower Gaufron and Sun Valley Farm overbridges were built, they would only have been expected to carry cart traffic. They show signs of having been rebuilt some years ago to cope with the increasing loads.

㉟ DOWN: The third of the three traditional whistle boards which are on this side reminds drivers of the approach to the three crossings at Neuadd (Hall) Farm. There is also another rarity: the yellow disc with the black outline of a conifer. This was originally to warn the drivers of steam trains that they were in an area susceptible to fires. The reverse of the sign is a yellow disc with a black diagonal stripe to advise drivers travelling in the opposite direction that the restriction has ended.

㊱ The encroaching forest restricts views for about a mile.

㊲ UP: The fire sign for up trains stands alongside Cwmbach Llechrhyd Bridge. Spanning the A470 Rhayader-Builth Wells road with a height restriction of 14 feet, it has been subject to too many 'bashes', resulting in a 10mph restriction for trains crossing the bridge.

Builth Road

Builth Wells is about two miles from the line and so the suffix 'Road' was appropriate, but Builth Road quickly became a village in its own right, growing around two railways, the Central Wales and Mid Wales Lines, which crossed each other at right angles. The lower level Mid Wales Line roughly followed the course of the River Wye.
The first station opened on the site was named Llechryd by the Mid Wales Railway. When the CWR opened a station it made the distinction by naming it Builth Road. It was not until 1889 that Llechryd also became Builth Road. There was appreciable interchange traffic and eventually a lift was installed between the two levels. The terms Low Level and High Level only came into use in 1950. The Low Level line closed on December 31st 1962, but the High Level designation remained in use for nearly another eight years. The track was double through the station.

UP: Most of the infrastructure was on this side. Now all that remains is the goods shed, currently a council depot, plus an inaccessible platform with a buffer stop. A row of terraced cottages housed the workers at this railway village and the stationmaster occupied the detached house at the southern end.

DOWN: The austere station building was once partly occupied by the HoWL engineers. Seen from the train it is at best functional but it is a little more impressive when viewed from further afield. With part of the brickwork painted white, a former doorway bricked up and a demarcation between ground and first floors where they were divided by a canopy, it would not win any awards. The removal of the three bay windows from the first floor, when it was converted into flats, has only added to the starkness. The low level station building is now the Cambrian Arms public house.

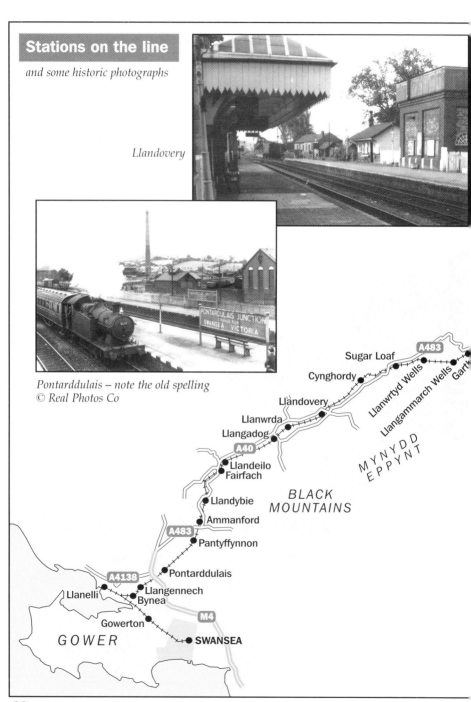

Stations on the line

and some historic photographs

Llandovery

Pontarddulais – note the old spelling
© Real Photos Co

Sugar Loaf
Cynghordy
Llandovery
Llanwrda
Llangadog
A40
Llandeilo
Fairfach
Llandybie
Ammanford
A483
Pantyffynnon
A4138
Pontarddulais
Llanelli
Llangennech
Bynea
Gowerton
GOWER
M4
SWANSEA

A483
Llanwrtyd Wells
Llangammarch Wells
Garth
MYNYDD
EPPYNT
BLACK
MOUNTAINS

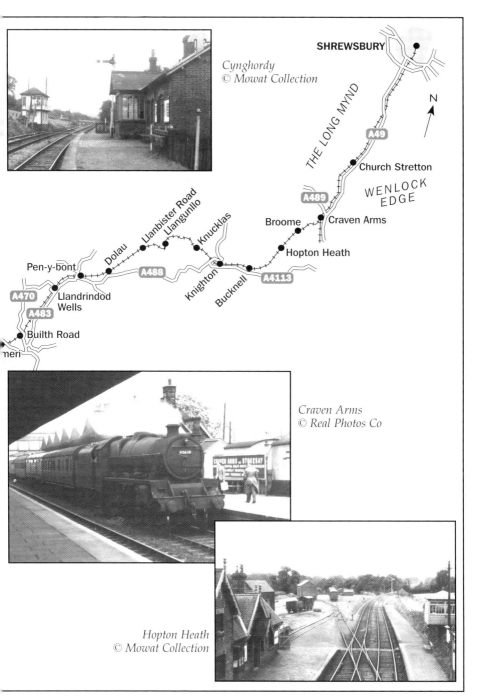

Cynghordy
© *Mowat Collection*

SHREWSBURY

THE LONG MYND

A49

N

Church Stretton

WENLOCK EDGE

A489

Broome • Craven Arms

Hopton Heath

Llanbister Road
Llangunllo

Knucklas

Dolau

Pen-y-bont

A488

Knighton

Bucknell

A4113

A470

Llandrindod
Wells

A483

Builth Road

meri

Craven Arms
© *Real Photos Co*

Hopton Heath
© *Mowat Collection*

UP: A timber yard now occupies the triangle where a curve once linked the LNWR to the Mid Wales Railway from Moat Lane Junction to Three Cocks Junction near Brecon. This curve saw frequent goods use but only occasional passenger services. The River Wye is partially hidden from view by trees as the train crosses it via an undistinguished girder bridge. At this point, the river has 280 feet to drop before it reaches the sea. The Wye Valley Walk follows the southern bank of the river. It passes beneath the bridge only 350 rail yards from Builth Road station but nearly five miles by footpath.

38 The railway now enters the old county of Brecknock (Breconshire) through a wooded area.

DOWN: Site of the former Rhosferig siding, used by freight trains awaiting access to Builth Road across the river. Here is the 64 yards' long Rhosferig tunnel. Afon Chwefri barely shows on the map as it meanders on its way to join the River Irfon shortly before the confluence with the River Wye at Builth Wells. To bridge it, the Central Wales Extension Railway constructed a splendid brick edifice which cannot be seen from the train. A large 30 feet high arch spans the river with a smaller one crossing a farm track. The depth of the bridge and supporting walls creates a tunnel-like atmosphere made more eerie by the surrounding tall trees.

39 Barely a minute after leaving Rhosferig Tunnel, the line enters the 115 yards long Cilmeri Tunnel which is crossed by the A483.

Cilmeri

The main feature of the village, a monolith erected to commemorate Llywelyn ap Gruffudd, the last native Prince of Wales, who was killed here in 1282, is to be seen on the up side 400 yards away close to a white bungalow. The station is reached from the village along an unmade lane, alongside the Prince Llywelyn Inn.

Cilmeri station opened as Cefn-y-Bedd – 'By the Grave' – in 1867, but it was quickly changed to Cilmery. In 1936, it was renamed Cilmery Halt, thought to be the first HoWL station to be demoted in this way, but several other minor stations were to receive the same status following the Beeching rationalisation. The term 'halt' remained until 1969 when it was deleted from the British Rail vocabulary, though it was not until 1980 that the Welsh spelling of the village was adopted.

For the next nine miles to Llanwrtyd Wells the line heads up the valley of the Irfon. The river is never far away, almost entirely on the Down side, on its way to join the Wye close to the Royal Welsh Showground at Builth Wells.

42 The B4519 Upper Chapel to Brecon Road is crossed.

Garth

The train slows for the station and the farm crossing beyond.

UP: A row of golden conifers borders the line in a garden where the householder has a private gate onto the platform. A car park has been created here and a replica Great Western spear fence erected. There are a handful of former railway cottages set back and the remnants of the old cattle dock platform are followed by a siding area. One of these used to lead to the brickworks in the village.

DOWN: For nearly a century there was a passing loop at Garth and the down platform remains. Pieces of the rough wall that encompassed the wooden waiting shelter can still be found. The first signal box was at the south end of the platform but was replaced between the wars by a box closer to Lewis Crossing.

43 Aberdulais Farm crossing is a metalled road in the true meaning of the word because the actual crossing of the track is on ribbed metal blocks instead of the more normal sleepers. The surveyors of the line must have been particularly frustrated at this point to find that they could not avoid having to bridge the River Irfon twice in a quarter of a mile. Their only consolation was that they appear to have been able to use duplicate drawings for the two bridges.

DOWN: The rolling Mynydd Eppynt overlooks the line. The absence of farm buildings is because it was depopulated at the outset of the Second World War when over fifty farmers had to evacuate the area for it to be turned into a military artillery range. It remains so to this day and the keen-eyed may spot the red warning flags that fly when firing is taking place. Walkers wanting to use the few public footpaths in the area will find the dates of firing displayed on local notice boards. The fifty-six yards long Llangammarch Tunnel has been bored through the top of a hill on a 1 in 80 climb.

DOWN: As the train leaves the tunnel, a rocky outcrop obscures the view of the barium well which gave the village its brief flirtation with tourism a century ago. A new generation is discovering the delights of the area attracted by its seclusion. The River Irfon and the Lake Hotel, one of the principal hotels in Mid Wales during the Victorian era, has recently seen a reversal in its fortunes, beyond may just be seen.

Llangammarch

The quiet village of Llangammarch Wells is one of the four Mid Wales spas to which the railway brought thousands of visitors during the Victorian and Edwardian eras. Before World War II, the village boasted every kind of tradesman together with a bank, police station and a school. Overlooked by its intimate church, it still has its post office, village store and, unusually, a secondhand bookshop. There is also a miniature riverside garden where the ducks rival those at Bucknell and the Aberceirios pub is nearby. Cross the river and follow it for a hundred yards or so and you will come to the Aberceiros Inn.

UP: There was a short siding on the opposite face of the single platform. The goods picked up from here often included spa water as this was the only one of the 'wells' whose water was suitable for bottling, though as with some other therapeutic mineral waters, they are said to have tasted very unpleasant on arrival!
The redbrick station building has long since succumbed to the ball and chain. The bridge beyond the station gives the appearance of having

36

been intended for double track, but this was due to the lie of the land rather than any grandiose expansion plans.

DOWN: A quiet caravan site stands where the River Cammarch joins the Irfon.

45 This is primrose territory. The HoWL has its charms throughout the year and those with the opportunity should travel it in all seasons, but here it is probably seen at its best in early Spring. The spectacle of lambs scurrying away from the train, the primroses, the hawthorn blossom, the trees still in bud have not obscured the distant hills, the nesting birds….

DOWN: The River Irfon almost laps the track as the Camddwr brook joins it from the north. The lane at Glancawddwr underbridge is the continuation of a Roman Road. Alongside a ford and just visible from the train is a most delightful footbridge. The designer must have eaten his tea from a willow pattern plate! On a hot summer's day this is perhaps the most idyllic spot along the entire ninety miles of the HoWL.

47 **DOWN**: Rail travellers always see the worst side of a building and the Abernant Hotel is no exception. Coach travellers are obliged to walk the last hundred yards to the hotel because their vehicle cannot pass beneath the bridge which has a 10 feet height restriction.

Llanwrtyd

Llanwrtyd Wells town centre is about a quarter of a mile from the station. It has a number of hotels, pubs and eating places, including a Michelin starred restaurant. Its political status allows Llanwrtyd Wells to describe itself as a town and as such it claims to be the smallest in Britain. It has certainly managed to capitalise on its position and achieves a status disproportionate to its size through tourism. The surrounding hills are rich with wildlife and in addition to the red kite, are also home to other species including curlews, ravens, buzzards and peregrine falcons. Special attractions include the annual nine day *Beer Festival* in November, the *Runners v Mountain Bikers v Horses Race* and, of course, the *World Bog Snorkelling Championship* – probably the only one of its kind!

Another prize winning station, in 2003 it shared a First Prize with Dolau in the Wales in Bloom competition and it is easy to see why. The improvements were originally carried out with funding from the Prince of Wales Trust and the gardens are now looked after by a local group. The station building has stepped extensions in various shades of blue brick at the southern end of the building, each lower and narrower than the part before. It is currently occupied by a bacon wholesalers. Outside the station, alongside a car park there is a paved picnic area and small garden overlooked by a delightful Station House.

48 This is the least altered of the five remaining passing loop stations.

DOWN: The station building has long gone. The platform is reached via a barrow crossing.

UP: The former goods shed has been extended and re-roofed. There were only two sidings, one alongside the through line, the other into the goods shed. A boundary fence now prevents access to the site of the two signal boxes, the 1928 replacement box being a few yards nearer to the station than the original. From 1966 it was relegated to the status of a ground frame before being closed in 1986. A grating is all that remains of the site of the water crane – a reminder of where steam trains replenished their tenders.

When the driver has obtained the Llandovery token, the train begins the 3 mile climb to Sugar Loaf summit at 1 in 70. The River Irfon is now crossed for the last time. As the train passes four more almost identical farm crossings, the climb eases to 1 in 80. The lie of the land means that while there are glimpses of the distant forests on the down side, little can be seen on the up.

49 Here are two crossings only five yards apart but on different farms.

After a farm overbridge, the train slows to 10mph for Berthddu open level crossing where visibility on the down approach is totally obscured by a cottage.

UP: Road and rail begin a parallel route to Llandovery. Unfortunately for the railway engineers, the way forward is also shared by seemingly innocuous streams, each of which requires a bridge, drain or culvert.

50 In steam days there were sand traps on both sides to catch any runaway wagons or locomotives. A passing loop installed here at the turn of the last century was extended during World War II to accommodate longer trains.

DOWN: As hills encompass the line, a digger can be seen half way up a track, apparently hard at work. It has been there for many years, quietly rusting.

Sugar Loaf

A low retaining wall is rapidly followed by a second which is all that remains of the former down platform – except that this was no ordinary platform. Sugar Loaf Summit, as the station was called when it opened in 1899, was restricted to use by the railway workers at this lonely outpost. It closed in 1965, but reopened for public use in 1984, although available only on summer Sundays. Now it is a request halt for all trains.

DOWN: At 820 feet above sea level the 1 in 80 climb converts to a 1 in 70 descent. The platform is only 60 feet long and as a single car unit is 75 feet long, it is necessary to leave or join the train through the forward door only. Only the foundations remain of the railway cottages which stood overlooking the station. They were not as remote as it might appear because, although there were few people in the area, the A483 passes within yards. Leaving the station, with its mass of willowherb, walkers should be aware that the route to the Sugar Loaf is alongside a dangerously fast stretch of road. However, there is a picnic spot and viewpoint on the Sugar Loaf, offering a superb view towards the Black Mountains and Llandovery.

There are twelve 'Sugar Loafs' listed in the Ordnance Survey Gazetteer of Great Britain, two of which are not so far away. One is 4 miles from the line at Penybont and the other 32 miles as the crow flies to the east, near Abergavenny.

Just beyond the station, a wall marks the spot where drivers of steam trains had to stop at a signal box to exchange tokens. The next bridge is described as an aqueduct which is perhaps an overstatement but it does carry a fast-flowing stream over the line in a conduit or trough attached to the south face. There was a catch point here to divert any runaway wagons intent on joining the single line through the tunnel.

51 The 1001-yards-long Sugar Loaf Tunnel takes the line through about 45 degrees on a falling gradient of 1 in 70. The southern mouth is 45 feet lower than the north.

Maintenance of the tunnel, planned or otherwise, has led to the line being closed several times. In 1926 there was a landslip at the north end and the scars can be still be seen today. The rock has been stepped back to the farm road which crosses just beyond the mouth. More serious was the closure in 1949 to repair the roof which had collapsed close to an old airshaft. In 1992, a concrete lining was applied at the northern end and this is clearly visible as the train enters the tunnel. Venturing over the top of the tunnel, the reason for the maintenance problems is obvious. A stream flows straight across from west to east and the rock-strewn ground is quite boggy. The area has been partially planted with conifers, but none have been allowed to grow along the line of the tunnel. The county boundaries of Powys and Carmarthenshire cross the line of the tunnel.

DOWN: Now follows what is considered to be the best view on the line with the train hugging the hillside for the descent from the tunnel, always assuming the weather is kind, because it is not unknown for sunshine at one end of the tunnel to give way to fog at the other! Looking backwards, the conical peak of Sugar Loaf takes shape. The next twenty miles are all downhill with the first four at 1 in 60, so any temptation to give the train its head has to be resisted as a series of curves means a maximum 45 mph. Numerous culverts take the many water courses which flow from Bryn Nichol (up) to Afon Wyddon and Afon Bran.

❷ Conifer plantations appear to dominate the distant hills but the line is actually passing through a tapestry of fields bounded by masses of deciduous trees.

DOWN: Passengers, especially those on the up side of the train, can be forgiven for leaping to their feet at this point. Ahead, as the line gently curves left, there is a glimpse of Cynghordy Viaduct. Completed in 1868, this architectural delight, enhanced by the magnificent scenery around, is built of sandstone with 18 brickline arches. The viaduct is 283 yards long and carries the train 102 feet above the Afon Bran on a 26 chains curve. The outer sides of the piers taper quite markedly. It almost appears to have been kit-built because numbers have been carved on the larger stones, but whatever, the result is heartlifting and one can only admire the engineering expertise of those who built it. In the shadow of the viaduct there is a chapel with its chapel house and a farm. These do not encroach under the viaduct as the land a few yards parallel to it has been pegged out with L & NW boundary signs – large metal pins hammered deep into the ground.

❻ An overbridge was built to link two sides of a farm dissected by the coming of the railway. The train now slows as it approaches Cynghordy station.

Cynghordy

The village of Cynghordy has evolved into a community with a number of centres. The school provides one which still draws together the families from the outlying farms, but the brickworks on the Cilycwm road was another, where the council built twenty houses to accommodate the workers' families. Cynghordy bricks were made from shale from the surrounding hills and were considered to be the best engineering bricks in the country. It must have been so, for in 1906, the brickworks was bought and modernised by a company from Leeds, when the beehive ovens were replaced by a modern building with a stack which was visible for miles around. Bricks were produced here for the construction of the railway. In fact at that time there were two brickworks in existence and the one in Glandwr Field near the viaduct probably provided the bricks which line the arches.

UP: This part of the line saw considerable service in its first fifty years but with passing places roughly three miles apart, operations were restricted by the existence of an eight mile single track section between Sugar Loaf Summit and Llandovery. Plans for a loop at Cynghordy were delayed and it it was not until 1929 that one was installed. A second platform was not considered necessary so the loop was used only by goods trains or non-stopping passenger trains.

DOWN: Cynghordy had a substantial station building with the usual railway accommodation and an integral signal box. When all of this was demolished, a wooden store shed which had existed from about 1892 was converted for use as a waiting shelter. Suffering from wet rot, at the age of 103, it was replaced by a British Rail suburban style waiting shelter in 1996, so the station has missed out on the more aesthetic shelters to be seen at other stations on the line.

UP: The top of the old rail fish van that stands by the crossing is one of dozens to be seen at farms throughout Mid Wales. Trains are required to slow to 10mph at the crossing. Unseen from the train, Penyparc

42

underbridge was constructed by a master craftsman using local bricks to create a superb example of the art of bricklaying.

56 **DOWN**: Since passing under the viaduct, the River Bran has turned southwards and now flows in the valley below the line, with the A483 road beyond at the edge of the Brecon Beacons. A bridge passes over the road towards Cilycwm close by the site of the former brickworks

57 A private farm bridge crosses the line between two fields, a long way from the nearest road. Many other minor farm crossings have been removed on the descent from Bryn Nicol. The line then crosses another Pen-y-bont Road via a classic brick- built bridge.

58 **DOWN**: With the start of the Towy Valley, the track levels for the first time since the approach to Llanwrtyd Wells. The church, Llanfair, which is without Llandovery can be reached via a footpath which crosses the line, but the steepness of the final climb means that most churchgoers are more likely to use the road. Across the town can be seen the tower of Llandingat, within Llandovery.

59 **UP**: The last Central Wales Extension Railway milepost stands tall. The track bed widens where the former Vale of Towy Railway is met end-on, 59 miles 13 chains from the junction at Craven Arms. You are now 29 miles from Llandeilo Junction near Llanelli.

29 Historically the up or London direction was southward from this point, but for the sake of simplicity the line is now designated up northbound and down southbound throughout. The normal route to London from Llandovery is via Swansea, but students of the timetable may find some interesting journey possibilities via Shrewsbury or Hereford.

DOWN: A girder bridge crosses Cilycwm Road and you then pass a school, public swimming pool and lorry yard before arriving at the full barrier level crossing over the A40 London to Fishguard road. The train stops here for the driver to pull a cord to operate the level crossing barriers before entering the station.

Llandovery

Llandovery is a market town with a charter that goes back more than 500 years. The dispensation to issue drinking licences within a 6 mile radius of the town was a privilege used by the Lord of the Manor to raise money for his coffers. Many licences were issued, but it was nothing to the number of outlets when Llandovery became a key stopping place on the drovers' route.

Station Road was renamed Queensway following the visit of the Queen by train in August 1955 when she came to open the Usk Reservoir. Llandovery was joint London & North Western and Great Western territory. The cream and green building was formerly the porters' lodge. The main building is part single storey, part double and constructed of granite. The platforms are very short, given the station's former status. A three road LNWR engine shed and immense water tower once dominated this area. The shed was larger than its Great Western counterpart because of the need for bigger engines to cope with the gradients to the north.

UP: Landscaped gardens now cover the site of the Great Western shed. When in use it was hidden by a tall water tower and wooden shelter. The water crane for locomotives was at the end of the platform ramp with the signal box alongside the level crossing. For up trains, the crossing gates are operated from a plunger on the platform.

Beyond a radio mast, a siding trails off the passing loop towards an engineers' platform. Nearby, the playing field of Llandovery College includes a par three golf course which is open to the public.

DOWN: As we leave the station armed with the token for Llandeilo, we get a brief view of the ruins of the Norman Castle on a mound in the centre of the town. The train continues virtually on the level along what has always been single track. The stand at Llandovery Rugby Club – the Drovers – can be seen.

UP: There is an attractive, riverside public footpath from the town towards the four span Llwynjack Bridge where, with no ballast between the sleepers, it is possible to stand and watch a train pass barely 3 feet overhead. A century ago, the bridge was moved a few yards upstream whilst the current replacement structure was built and when the river level is low, parts of the temporary pier supports can be seen alongside. Cow parsley and willowherb brighten the area in summer and help to hide the gravel pit.

The river follows a decidedly meandering course and the whole area is susceptible to flooding. The line is about three feet proud of the flood plain, which allows travellers a better view than might otherwise have been the case.

28 Over the next few miles there is a series of almost identical crossings and livestock creeps, usually in pairs, the crossings providing access when the creeps are impassable. Some of the creeps do not easily accommodate modern tractors, so if need be the farmer can go over the top, leaving the livestock to go underneath.

The Black Mountains can be seen to the east of the line.

Llanwrda

The village of Llanwrda is just over a quarter of a mile away. A classic post office/shop is at its heart and opposite it is a garage where a number of interesting railway artefacts are displayed. It is not unknown for visitors to mistake it for a station!

26 The train slows to 10mph in advance of an open level crossing.

DOWN: The platforms were staggered and the disused down side is in advance of the crossing. The road only goes a few yards over the crossing towards a former public house.
Southbound trains stop only on request but northbound trains are required to stop at the single platform and 'whistle before proceeding'.

㉕ DOWN: The River Towy seems determined to come into conflict with the railway because it is never more than a few yards away over the next mile. It succeeds in its apparent attempt to breech the railway embankment at the 93 yard long Towy Viaduct.

Llangadog

Llangadog is a charming village nestled around a Norman Church with an interesting blend of architecture including Georgian and Victorian. Turn right out of the station and it is not far before you come to the Telegraph pub. For the village centre, continue up the road where there is a post office and other stores, as well as five more pubs, all within yards of each other. Six miles from Llandovery, at the time that the Lord of the Manor was dispensing licences, Llangadog was overseen by the Bishop and it did not take long for him to get the same idea for raising money!

㉔ There were sidings here on both sides of the line.

UP: Note the garage where Thomas has been for longer than he has been a tank engine. A modern, ungated level crossing crosses the A4069.

The up platform remains in use – the down platform and passing loop having been removed. There was once a building here similar to that on the up platform at Llandrindod and were it still here, it could be used by the engineers in place of the rather less than attractive portakabins that are here now.

The creamery – once rail-connected – dominates the down side. It produces award winning Welsh salted butter and a variety of luxury canned dairy goods as well as UHT and powdered milk.

The line crosses another River Bran, one of three to be found on O.S. Landranger map 146, but this one is crossed by an insignificant girder bridge and is even less distinguished than that which is graced by the Cynghordy Viaduct.

UP: A few yards downstream, a bridge once carried a short private siding into the dairy. An unusual feature of the field here is that it is bordered on three sides by three different rivers, the Towy, Sawdde and Bran, and on the fourth by the railway. The Sawdde Bridge is very similar to that at Llwynjack. The Sawdde flows into the Towy about 200 yards to the west (up).

㉓ At 6.25 am on 19th October 1987, a two-car diesel train from Swansea plunged from Glanrhyd bridge into the River Towy. Much swollen by heavy rain, the river had scoured the bed around the central support causing it to collapse. In the darkness the driver had no warning of the danger ahead and very sadly, he and three of the ten passengers on board were drowned. The new bridge may not be elegant, but it is functional and imposing. It is followed by a 10mph restriction for the ungated level crossing at Glanrhyd.

UP: Glanrhyd was the first of four HoW Line stations closed in the 1950s. It had been opened in 1858, closed in 1931 and reopened in 1938. Apart from the recent addition of a porch over the front door, which opens onto the platform, the station house is unchanged.

Across the valley stands a redbrick house which was once a boarding school for young girls. Many arrived at the station by train and were greeted by the stationmaster and his wife When they walked into Llandeilo, they would walk along the line – how things have changed!

The line is almost straight for the next 3 miles to the outskirts of Llandeilo while the river meanders in the same general direction. In the worst of the weather, despite the presence of a series of groynes, the river floods the surrounding fields and it is not unusual for the train to appear to cross a large lake.

㉒ DOWN: About a mile away across the Towy and, appropriately, to the east is the village of Bethlehem where Christmas cards can be specially franked at the post office.

㉑ UP: The site of Talley Road station with a farm building and bungalow close to the line obscuring the Station House, this being one of the few farmhouses close to the line in the Towy Valley as most are beside the A40 in the lee of the hill. A coal yard hut is set well back from the line where there was once a small loop, which at least gave some justification for the station. Though 6 miles away, the station was named after the village of Talley with its ruined abbey, rather than after the nearby village of Manordeilo, despite the fact that the best route to the railway from Talley has always been the road (B4302) to Llandeilo.

⓴ Ahead is Llandeilo. Overhead it is often possible to see one of the Red Kites which have been successfully extending their habitat from the upper Towy Valley. Besides their colour, they are distinguished by their angular wings and forked tails.

Llandeilo

Llandeilo is a delightful, hospitable town with a reputation for original arts and crafts, much of it produced locally. Newton House is a National Trust property open to the public. The parkland at Dinefwr Park was designed by Capability Brown and a grove of trees planted by him leads to a classic Victorian bandstand which can be seen from the line. The remains of Dinefwr Castle stand out on a bluff. With historic landmarks like this, as well as a High Street full of interesting shops, pubs and hotels, it is well worth the walk up the hill from the station.

⓳ UP: The siding here has seen little use for at least a decade.

DOWN: Here was Llandeilo North signal box and the wasteland betrays the site of the former sidings. Any opportunity to improve the station area following the demolition of the derelict station buildings and signal box in 1996 has been blighted by the lack of a decision as to whether an eastern town by-pass is to follow the route of the railway and cross the flood plain to Ffairfach.

UP: Partially covered by gravel are some rails, the remnants of a siding which once led to a small shed behind the main station building. There was also a siding which ran parallel to the station approach road. A more direct route to and from the town centre for pedestrians is via steps and a steep, roughly-laid brick path.

At the end of the 19th century, an impressive two storey station building extended along much of the length of the up platform. Even the drainpipes were embossed with the Prince of Wales' feathers. The steps of early LNWR carriages used to be set quite low, hence the low section platform. When the design of carriages changed, it was impractical to raise the lower section because of the station buildings. These days, diesel units are required to stop at the higher level.

DOWN: Access to the platform is via a barrow crossing. In 1955, a signal box was built here using bricks from the Cynghordy works. It replaced the North, South and Carmarthen Junction boxes and closed in September 1986. The eastern face of the platform used to be a bay for the Carmarthen service, which travelled via a line through Golden Grove and Llanarthne. A footpath leads to a suspension bridge and riverside walk.

The token having been obtained for the section to Pantyffynnon, our journey continues.

⓲ UP: Despite appearances to the contrary, the fourth and final crossing of the River Towy only ever carried a single track. It often goes unnoticed when the eye is drawn to the single row of houses on Bridge Street (A483) with the Church tower above and though individually these dwellings may not appear to have much architectural merit, artists have long appreciated their delightful quality as they step down one by one from the town towards the river. Built in 1848, the road bridge was considered to be one of the wonders of wales. A major engineering feat, designed and built by local craftsmen of local stone, it has a meadow in the foreground and is backed by Dynevor Park, providing one of the most memorable views on the route.

DOWN: River Cennen flows into the Towy from the South. The line follows the valley of this river and crosses it four times in the next three miles as it climbs to the minor summit at Derwydd Road.

Ffairfach

Separated by the Towy, Ffairfach (meaning little fair) retains its own distinct identity despite its close proximity to Llandeilo. The two stations are less than a mile apart.

UP: For a century there was a private siding into the gasworks close to the station.

DOWN: A basic, single platform runs alongside the former station house. Down trains have to stop short of the crossing for the conductor to operate the road traffic lights, but in the up direction, trains only stop at the station on request because they activate the lights by a treadle and can cross the road at 10mph. Until 1960, there was a Co-operative Dairy beyond the crossing, but the sidings were removed three years after its closure. The former signal box was moved to the Gwili Railway, north of Carmarthen.

㉗ The scene changes to woodland as the Afon Cennen flows a few yards from the line.

㉖ UP: Partially hidden is a picturesque ford close to the track at Meusydd Mill.

DOWN: The Cennen Valley meets the line at right angles allowing more views of the distant Black Mountains and a brief glimpse of Carreg Cennen Castle about three miles away.

⑮ DOWN: A few trees straddle the summit of the climb at 229 feet above sea level just beyond Derwydd Road overbridge, obscuring the former railway properties at the closed station, which is identified by some coal staithes. For over forty years, Derwydd Road had three

platforms, the up being an island, and was the only station in the 8 miles between Llandeilo and Pantyffynnon where two passenger trains could cross. The others – Ffairfach, Llandybie and Ammanford/Tirydail – each had only one platform.
It is now downhill all the way to the sea.

At Cilyrychen the line crosses the A483 for a second time on the level.

⑭ UP: Cilyrychen limestone kilns were designed by R.K. Penson, the brother of T.K. Penson, the architect of Shrewsbury station buildings. Once the largest limestone quarry in Europe, it was the scene of substantial railway activity until the sidings, barely 400 yards long and officially known as the Limestone Branch, closed in 1969.
Llandybie Church now comes into view.

Llandybie

Llandybie was an industrial village, but recently the cluster of houses around the Norman Church have been renovated and a 16th Century pub, the Red Lion, is a pleasing watering hole for the traveller.

DOWN: There was once a passing loop, used only by goods trains. Down trains have to slow to 15mph for the open level crossing.

UP: Apart from a shelter, the single platform is now devoid of buildings. This is another station which is a request stop in one direction, but a full stop in the other as up trains stop for the conductor to operate the crossing. The locally-made name boards replicate a Great Western design but have been repainted black and white.

⑬ The train slows for Brynmarlais level crossing, which is surrounded by new bungalows.

⑫ An underbridge which has a height restriction of only 7 feet 9 inches takes the lane leading to Aberlash Mill (up) under the line. The line crosses the River Loughor which it then follows to the sea.

UP: Some factory units are set well back and the intervening road now occupies the position of the Mountain Branch which led principally to Cross Hands but also to the Llandybie Lime Works. An engineers' cabin stands on the site of the Duffryn platform.

Ammanford

Ammanford is the largest town on the line apart from Swansea and Shrewsbury. It was a centre for anthracite mining and a busy industrial centre and the Great Western Hotel is a reminder of that bygone era. Successfully adapting to a post industrial age, Ammanford's shopping centre is within a half mile walk of the station, as are the sporting venues for rugby, cricket and tennis, and both indoor and outdoor bowls.

DOWN: This station was named Tirydail when it opened at the end of the 19th Century. At the time, Ammanford station was a mile away on the branch to Brynaman. When that closed to passengers in 1958, 'Tirydail' became 'Ammanford and Tirydail', but with the nationwide purge of dual names, 'Tirydail' was dropped. Nevertheless, the level crossing at Ammanford station is known as Tirydail crossing! It has full barriers which reflects the volume of traffic in the area. Rhydaman, the Welsh for Ammanford, was added to the nameboard a decade ago.

⑪ DOWN: After the Leisure Centre and immediately beyond the bridge, was Parcyrhun Halt. This platform was opened in 1936 principally for the miners who worked at the complex of nearby collieries. It closed in 1955.

UP: Opposite the halt was the start of a maze of lines to the numerous collieries. It is still possible to trace many of them and the last branch survived until the closure of the Wernos Colliery Washery in 1988. The double track section through Pantyffynnon began at the point where the Loughor laps the line again. This wide-open space once rang to the clunking of coal wagons being shunted.

DOWN: There was room for only one siding where terraced houses back up to the line. Ahead, the first semaphore signal for 78 miles protects a level crossing.

UP: A car park stands where branches once headed across the Loughor to the Pantyffynnon and Wernos collieries.

Pantyffynnon

The road at Pantyffynnon narrows to single file over one of the few remaining manually operated gated crossings in the country. It is controlled by a keeper using a key obtained from a cupboard on the platform, the key being released electrically by the signalman at the nearby box.

UP: Another semaphore signal protects the crossing. The disused platform has been converted into a prize-winning garden by signalmen past and present.

DOWN: Beyond the rugby field there is a suspension bridge over the River Amman. The one remaining branch line along the HoWL avoids the platform as it skirts the station on the way to Gwaun-Cae-Gurwen, six miles away. A trainman-operated level crossing is visible on the branch just beyond the station. The branch currently is out of use.

DOWN: The signal box stands just beyond the junction. A stop is made here to exchange the Llandeilo token. The line continues as a single-track, tokenless block section for another 5 miles to Hendy Junction, this section being controlled from the signalling centre at Port Talbot.

Pantyffynnon South signal box was built in 1892 to replace one which stood on the other side of the track. At the time a short loop went behind the old box to Dynevor Works. The 'South' was dropped when its sister box closed in 1966. Officially a Type 5, it is one of the commonest of the numerous different designs constructed by the GWR. Shortly after passing the signal box, the line crosses the river Amman at its confluence with the Loughor.

❿ UP: On the parapet of the bridge over the Amman is a concrete slab inscribed 'L.R.&D.Co Oct 1838 – Oct 1871'. The Llanelly Railroad and Dock Company constructed this part of the line from its port to Llandeilo. The Great Western Railway took over responsibility for it when the river was diverted and the bridge rebuilt. The line stands a few feet above the flood plain and crosses a series of arches.

DOWN: A two aspect colour light signal controls trains near the last of the semaphore signals for up trains. A signal box here oversaw a branch to Garn Mill Colliery until it was closed in the early years of the century.

❾ The River Loughor comes near to the track again. At times when the weather is grey and misty, this marshy landscape has a Dickensian feel to it.

❽ UP: A small signal box was opened at Tyn-y-Cerrig crossing alongside milepost 7 in 1876. In 1905, a passing loop was installed before the section was doubled in 1907 and the box was moved a few yards to the south. It was closed in 1913.

❼ DOWN: A private siding to Glynhir tinplate works opened in 1911, but was removed in 1964.

❻ DOWN: Around Talyfan overbridge, the trees help to camouflage the Corus Coated Metals Works, once the Glamorgan Tinplate Works. A solitary siding stood here when it was connected to the railway.

Pontarddulais

UP: The site of the North signal box.

DOWN: Sidings covered what is now an expanse of rough ground and as a hawthorn hedge curves gently to the left, birch trees can be seen growing where was once the direct line to Swansea Victoria. Although closed to passengers in 1964, this line remained open as a single-track freight line as far as Grovesend Colliery for another 10 years. It was finally closed following the construction of a new connection from the colliery onto the Swansea District Line.

It is just possible to see the face of the 'from Swansea' platform but the 'to Swansea' platform has been dismantled. It is hard now to envisage that this was once a busy junction station where passengers could change for Swansea or Llanelli. An extensive building with waiting rooms and 'the usual offices' stood on a wide 'V' shaped centre platform. The former goods depot is now a garage.

A wooden GWR junction signal box stood in the centre of the 'from Llanelli' platform until December 1967. The platform remained in situ until 1996 when it was removed as part of a flood alleviation scheme in a further attempt to contain the River Loughor within its banks when in spate. Previous efforts had already led to the tract of land that was once occupied by the up sidings being bulldozed and planted.

The train now uses what was Platform 3.

The line crosses the River Loughor immediately ahead of the 88 yard long Pontarddulais tunnel which was originally constructed in 1838 to give the Llanelly Railroad & Dock Co access to the nearby coalfield. The line here was little more than a tramway at the time and so the tunnel has a very restricted width. From the station it looks as though an approaching train will not get through, but in fact there are several inches to spare on either side and a 20mph speed limit prevents any undue wobble. The track through the tunnel is laid on concrete to limit flood damage.

❺ **DOWN**: a three aspect colour light with a left 'feather' controls Hendy Junction, where a little-used double track connection to the Swansea District Line branches off.

The M4 motorway towers over the line at the head of the Loughor estuary.

DOWN: The Loughor Viaduct catches the eye just beyond Morlais

Junction on the Swansea District Line.

UP: What is now scrub land used to be a hive of railway activity with sidings around the defunct Morlais Colliery which mined coal from beneath the estuary.

❹ **DOWN**: Rail traffic was once so heavy here that when the Swansea District Line was created in 1913, a fly-under was constructed. Down trains used to veer to the left to pass beneath the District Line before joining it to the south of the Morlais Junction. The bridges over a path from Bryn-y-Mawr farm and the diversionary route can be seen.

DOWN: The junction signal box used to be situated between the down HoWL and the District Line. Since the closure of the fly-under, HoWL trains now join the up track of the Swansea District Line for about 100 yards before crossing to the down line. The original line from here was that of the Llanelly Railway & Dock Company which became part of what was known as the Central Wales and is now called the Heart of Wales Line. Consequently milepost **0** on the HoWL is at Llandeilo Junction and mileposts on the Swansea District Line – which was used principally by Fishguard boat trains and freight trains avoiding the Swansea bottleneck - finish at Morlais Junction.

UP: The bridge over the River Morlais carried a third track in the form of a passing loop which gave access to various sidings.

DOWN: The mean high tide mark is about 300 yards away, but flooding is not uncommon. The sewage works which can be seen at the water's edge, is protected!

UP: The scattering of houses and workshops are in Llangennech.

DOWN: Looking back we see the Loughor Viaduct with the motorway beyond.

Llangennech

❸ The station on what is now the up platform at Llangennech opened on the then single track line in 1839.

UP: There is a wide expanse of land either side of the line as it begins a gentle curve to the east alongside a recreation ground where once there were more than two tracks

DOWN: The track is now within yards of the estuary and many of the culverts have tidal flaps which are forced closed by the sea to prevent water flooding back towards the village. Though hard to identify nowadays, this was once the site of a small dock. Coal mined in the Llangennech collieries was initially brought to the dock by the Llangennech canal and later by a tramroad. This dock area is now frequently the site of fishing competitions. In the 19th Century it was also a 'seaside' destination for day trippers by train from Swansea.

UP: On the brow of the bend, a facing point took a spur to the Morlais Tinplate works, Llangennech Works, a sawmill, the inland collieries already mentioned and, latterly, the Royal Naval Supply Depot.

❷ DOWN: Looking back, there is another fine view of the Loughor Viaduct at Morfa Mawr with the backdrop of Cefn Drum. Ahead, on the South Wales main line and beyond a road bridge, can be seen the unique wooden Loughor Bridge.

Bynea

DOWN: As the line straightens on the approach to Bynea station, a gap in the lineside bushes gives a clue to the position of the Yspitty branch, a half mile of track which gave access to St. David's Tinplate Works. It originally joined what was a passing loop before the line was doubled. The first platform at Bynea stood on the loop, not the through line. At the time there was a level crossing at the western end and the old road is still used on either side of the line. An odd feature is what appears to be a false tunnel, but was in fact part of the original bridge.

❶ UP: At the old brickworks there were several sidings.

DOWN: The Genwen colliery branch was of such little importance that it closed in the middle of the Great War. The signal box which controlled it was a few chains beyond the spur to Techan Fach Colliery. The latter remained in use for the storage of wagons until the late fifties and can still be walked almost up to the main line. The train now curves to the left along a route first laid in 1913.

UP: The original route at Genwen Junction went straight ahead and now provides access to the Trostre Tinplate Works. Scrub land separates the old and new stretches of the HoWL before it joins the South Wales Main Line. The official 0 marker stands in front of a sign proclaiming 'Llandeilo Junction', 223 miles from London Paddington. The train now travels westwards along the South Wales Main Line for one mile into Llanelli. This line was originally built to 'broad' gauge (7 feet 0 inches) specifications by Isambard Kingdom Brunel but was converted to 'standard' gauge (4 feet 8½ inches) in 1872 which was 20 years before the final demise of the broad gauge.

DOWN: Look out for the tiled roof of the Penclacwydd Wildlife and Wetlands Centre – a mecca for those interested in wild birds where they can see a variety of migratory species visiting the estuary. On the opposite bank can be seen the houses of Penclawdd, an important centre for the production and preparation of Welsh cockles.

Llanelli

Until the middle of the last century, Llanelli prospered through its trade in coal, tinplate, copper, chemicals, manufacturing and pottery. Tinplate was once a key industry, and there were so many small tinplate works in Llanelli that it was known as 'Tinopolis'and the famous saucepans gave the town its 'Sospan' nickname. The first UK canned beer was produced in Llanelli by the local Felinfoel brewery using tinplate from the Trostre Tinplate Works. Trostre is a major local employer, though automation and the increased use of plastics for packaging have reduced the number of people employed there.

The town is reinventing itself as a centre for the media with a large TV studio in the town – and for tourism. The station is a ten minute walk from the town centre, which with its modern St. Elli shopping arcade and street markets on Thursdays and Saturdays, draws shoppers from a wide area.

For both locals and tourists, the most significant development has been the creation of the 21 kilometre Millennium Coastal Park, including the Wetlands Centre, cycleways, footpaths, fishing lakes and other attractions.

The train reverses directon here, so the driver and conductor exchange positions. The train passes Llandeilo Junction in the direction of Swansea along another 5 miles of single track line. The decision to remove the second track was a false economy as it now severely restricts railway operations in west Wales.

Technically the UP side is now on the left because on the South Wales Main Line, London is in that direction.

222 Motorists have an excellent view of the wooden structure of the Loughor rail bridge. Loughor station, which had been built here on the site of a Roman fort, closed in April 1960.

Gowerton

220 The supports of the bridge at the western end of the station used to carry the line from Pontarddulais via Swansea Bay to Swansea Victoria. This otherwise undistinguished station is now a request stop for Heart of Wales Line trains, catering mainly for locals going into Swansea. However, the platform can take a full length High Speed Train and charters which called here in August 1998 and July 1999 caused great excitement!

218 The former Cockett station can just be seen as the double track resumes ahead of the 788 yard long tunnel. Brunel faced considerable engineering difficulties here and the train passes under several supporting buttresses which he built to stabilise the cutting.

219 The line now descends sharply towards Swansea. At Swansea Loop West, a now single-track connection leads to the main line towards Paddington, avoiding Swansea station. Landore maintenance depot is on the left. At Swansea Loop East, the line from Llanelli joins the main line. Maliphant sidings lie to the east of the passenger line. Just before the station platforms, a staff car park is sited where a single line connection headed above the streets on embankments to the docks, emerging at the rear of the former L&NWR terminus at Swansea Victoria. The train now moves gently to a halt at Swansea High Street station, 121 miles from Shrewsbury.

Swansea

Swansea is a terminal station known as 'High Street' until the closure of Victoria. The Pontarddulais to Swansea Victoria section closed in June 1964, but the coastal and Clyne Valley paths make walking or cycling the former route easy as far as Gowerton.

With a population of 168,000, Swansea is the largest place on the line. Still a major port, it has many attractive beaches and a covered market renowned for its fresh fish and vegetables, cockles and laverbread. Other places to visit are the Glynn Vivian Art Gallery and a 1930s style Civic Centre with the world famous Brangwyn Panels. At Singleton Park there is an attractive botanical garden.

If you plan to explore the Swansea area – and there's a lot to see and enjoy – you can get a bus immediately outside the rail station which takes you to the bus station and the Quadrant shopping centre. A short walk takes you to the Marina, the Industrial and Maritime Museum and the golden sands of Swansea Bay.

A FEW WORDS OF WELSH

You will find on your travels that a knowledge of Welsh will be beneficial. You will also notice that the Welsh alphabet is different. Here are some examples which will help with the pronunciation:

ch = as in Scots loch
dd = th as in then
f = f as in of
ff = f as in off
ll = hl
rh = hr
si, su = sh as in shop
tsi = ch as in church

and then there are the extra vowels 'w' and 'y'

w = oo as in look, boot
y = it depends where it is in the word. If the word has one syllable, it is 'i' as in bin, but with more than one syllable it is pronounced like but, and then there are exceptions to these rules.

Many of the stations along the line start with 'Llan' so to know its meaning puts all those names into context. Originally describing an enclosure, it then came to mean a church and the surrounding area. It is usually followed by the name of a saint, but not always! Here is a list of many of the stations on the line:

Tref y clawdd (Knighton)   The town on the dyke
Cnwclas   Knucklas
Dolau   Meadows
Pen-y-bont   Bridgend
Llandrindod   Church of the Trinity
Buallt (Builth)   Cow pasture

Cilmeri	Recess of brambles
Garth	Headland or enclosure
Llangammarch	Church on River Camarch (march=horse)
Cynghordy	House of meeting or assembly
Llanymddyfri (Llandovery)	Church among the waters
Llanwrda	Church of the good man
Llangadog	Church of St. Cadog
Llandeilo	Church of St. Teilo
Ffairfach	Small fair
Llandybie	Church of St. Tybie
Rhydaman (Ammanford)	Ford on the River Amman
Pantyffynnon	Hollow of the well
Pontarddulais	Bridge over the River Dulais (black water)
Llangennech	Church of St. Cennech
Llanelli	Church of St. Elli
Abertawe (Swansea)	Mouth of the River Tawe

Here are a few more words you may come across on your travels:

Afon	– river
Bach, fach	– small
Ban, fan	– peak, crest
Blaen	– head, end, source
Bryn	– hill
Bwlch	– pass
Cefn	– ridge
Coch, goch	– red
Craig, graig	– rock
Croeso	– welcome
Cwm	– valley
Dinas	– city
Du, ddu	– black
Dyffryn	– valley
Eglwys	– church
Gorsaf	– station
Gwesty	– hotel, guest house

Glyn	– glen
Heol	– road
Llan	– church
Llwyn	– grove, bush
Llyn	– lake
Maen	– stone
Mawr, fawr	– great, big
Moel, foel	– bare hill
Mynydd, fynnydd	– mountain
Pentre	– village, homestead
Plas	– hall, mansion
Pont, bont	– bridge
Rheilffordd	– railway
Siop	– shop
Stryd	– street
Toiledau	– toilets (merched = ladies; dynion = gents)
Trên	– train
Tŷ	– house
Uchaf	– upper, higher, highest
Ystrad	– valley floor

And a few greetings:

Bore da	– good morning
Prynhawn da	– good afternoon
Noswaith dda	– good evening
Nos da	– goodnight
Sut mae?	– how are you?
Diolch	– thanks
Croeso	– welcome
Da	– good
Da iawn	– very good
Iechyd da!	– good health!
Esgusodwch fi	– excuse me

In all languages there are words that do not directly translate. One that springs instantly to mind is '*hwyl*'. I have seen it described as meaning 'cheers' but it can also be your mood – good or bad! It can be a feeling of joy which is almost spiritual, that feeling of uplift on a beautiful day – and there is plenty of *hwyl* when Wales wins a rugby match, but if they lose, it's *hwyl ddrwg*!

Approaching Llanwrda, by the Afon Tywi. Bill Meadows.